Going to See Santa

A TODDLER PREP™ BOOK

Ready
SetPrep

About Toddler Prep™ Books

The best way to prepare a child for any new experience is to help them understand what to expect beforehand, according to experts. And while cute illustrations and fictional dialogue might be entertaining, little ones need a more realistic representation to fully understand and prepare for new experiences.

With Toddler Prep™ Books, a series by ReadySetPrep™, you can help your child make a clear connection between expectation and reality for all of life's exciting new firsts. Born from firsthand experience and based on research from leading developmental psychologists, the series was created by Amy and Aaron Pittman — parents of two who know (all too well) the value of preparation for toddlers.

We're going to see Santa Claus! What a fun day. Let's talk about what happens when we see Santa.

Before Christmas, we go see Santa to take a picture and tell him what you want for Christmas!

First, we pick out a special outfit. We want to look our best for Santa.

When you're dressed and ready to go, we get in the car and drive to Santa.

Santa is so excited to see you! He travels from his home at the North Pole to visit us.

Santa goes to lots of different places to visit children.
He goes to Christmas parties...

...churches...

...and even shopping malls!

When we go to see Santa, there are lots of people there. We get in line and wait patiently for our turn.

Santa's space is decorated to look like the North Pole. There's pretend snow, presents, and a pretty Christmas tree with sparkly lights!

There's also a photographer with a big camera. Their job is to take your picture with Santa.

Sometimes we see Santa's elves! They are there to help Santa.

Santa Claus has a white beard, hat, and wears a big red suit and black boots.

When you go to see Santa, you sit on his lap. Santa is very nice and he's so happy to meet you.

If you don't want to sit on his lap, you can stand next to him.

It's ok if you're a
little nervous—
you can look
at me. I stay
with you all the
time.

19

Santa might say, "Ho, ho, ho!"—That's how Santa laughs! Let's practice our ho, ho, hos together!

Then, Santa will ask you what you want for Christmas. Do you want a new game? A toy truck? A stuffed animal?

Now it's time to take a picture with Santa!

22

Smile! This is a special picture we keep for a really long time.

After your picture, you hop off Santa's lap, wave goodbye, and say "Thank you!"

Then we go home and get ready for Christmas!